Aesch-Mezareph
or
Purifying Fire.

Hochlöblichr Kayserlichr Majestat Rhat, So der Wohledle Herr Schulteis mit recht.
In Franckfurt zeigt das Wapn und Löw geart; Führt, Johann Martin Baur v Eysenceck.

Knorr von Rosenroth

I

CHAPTER I

Elisha was a most notable prophet, an example of natural wisdom, a despiser of riches, (as the history of the healing of Naaman showeth, 2 Kings, c.5, v.16) and therefore truly rich. According to what is said in Pirke Aboth, viz., Who is rich? He that rejoiceth in his portion, cap. 4. For so the true physician of impure metals hath not an outward show of riches, but is rather like the Tohu of the first Nature, empty and void. Which word is of equal number with the word Elisha, viz., 411. For it is a very true saying in Baba Kama, fol. 71. col. 2. The thing which causeth riches, (such as natural wisdom) is supplied instead of riches.

Learn therefore to purify Naaman, coming from the north, out of Syria, and acknowledge the power of Jordan: Which is as it were Jar-din that is the River of Judgment flowing out of the north.

And remember that which is said in Baba Bathra, fol. 25, col. 2. He that will become wise, let him live in the South; and he that will grow rich, let him turn himself toward the north, etc. Although in the same place Rabbi Joshua Ben Levi says, let him live always in the south, for whilst be becomes wise, at the same time he becomes rich. "Length of Days is in her right hand, and in her left, Riches and Honour." Prov., c.3, v.16. So thou wilt not desire other riches.

But know, that the mysteries of this wisdom, differ not from the superior mysteries of the Kabalah. For such as is the consideration of the predicaments in holiness, the same is also in impurity; and the same Sephiroth which are in Atziluth, the same are in Assiah, yea, the same in that kingdom, which is commonly called the mineral kingdom; although their excellency is always greater upon the spiritual plane. Therefore the metallic root here possesseth the place of Kether, which hath an occult nature, involved in great obscurity, and from which all metals have their origin; even as the nature of Kether is hidden, and the other Sephiroth flow from thence.

Lead hath the place of Chokmah, because Chokmah immediately proceeds from Kether, as it immediately comes from the metallic root, and in enigmatic similes, it is called the "father" of the following natures.

Tin possesseth the place of Binah, shewing age, by its greyness, and shadowing forth severity and judicial rigour, by its crackling.

Silver is placed under the Classis of Chesed, by all the masters of the Kabalah, chiefly for its colour and use.

Thus far the white natures. Now follow the red.

Gold is placed under Geburah, according to the most common opinion of the Kabalists; Job in c.37, v.22, also tells us that gold cometh from the north, not only for its colour, but for the sake of its heat and sulphur.

Iron is referred to Tiphereth, for he is like a man of war, according to Exod., c.15, v.2, and hath the name of "Seir Anpin", from his swift anger, according to Psalm 2, v.ult., "kiss the son lest he be angry."

Netzach and Hod are the two median places of the body, and the seminal receptacles, and refer to the hermaphroditic brass. So also the two pillars of the Temple of Solomon (referring to these two Sephiroth) were made of brass, I Kings, c.7, v.15.

Jesod is argent vive. For to this, the name "living" is characteristically given; and this living water is in every case the foundation of all Nature and of the metallic art.

But the true medicine of metals is referred to Malkuth, for many reasons; because it represents the rest of the natures under the metamorphoses of Gold and Silver, right and left, judgment and mercy, concerning which we will speak more largely elsewhere.

Thus I have delivered to thee the key to unlock many secret gates, and have opened the door to the inmost adyta of Nature. But if anyone hath placed those things in another order, I shall not contend with him, inasmuch as all systems tend to the one truth.

For it may be said, the three supernals are the three fountains of metallic things. The thick water is Kether, salt is Chokmah, and sulphur is Binah; for known reasons. And so the seven inferior will represent the seven metals, viz., Gedulah and Geburah, Silver and Gold; Tiphereth, Iron; Netzach and Hod, Tin and Copper; Jesod, Lead; and Malkuth will be the metallic woman, and the Luna of the wise men; and the field into which the seeds of secret minerals ought to be cast, that is the water of Gold, as this name (Mezahab) occurs, Genesis, c.36, v.39.

But know, my Son, that such mysteries are hid in these things as no tongue may be permitted to utter. But I will not offend any more with my tongue, but will keep my mouth with a bridle, Psalm 39, v.2.

Gehazi the Servant of Elisha, is the type of the vulgar students of Nature, who contemplate the valley and depths of Nature, but do not penetrate into her secrets.

Hence they labour in vain, and remain servants for ever. They give counsel about procuring the son of the wise men whose generation exceeds the power of Nature, but they can add nothing to assist in his generation, 2 Kings, c.4, v.14 (for which purpose a man like Elisha is required). For Nature doth not open her secrets to them, v.26, but contemns them, v.30, and the raising of the dead is impossible to them, v.31. They are covetous, cap. 5, v.20;

liars, v.22; deceivers, v.25; prattlers of other men's deeds, 2 Kings, c.8, v.4-5, and instead of riches, contract a leprosy themselves, that is disease, contempt and poverty, v.27. For the word Gehazi, and the word Chol, profane or common, have both the same number.

CHAPTER II

In metallic things, Geburah is of the class to which Gold is referred; which has again its decad ; (i.e., ten orders or degrees). So that,

1. Chethem, that is, pure fine Gold, is referred to the Kether thereof; which, Canticles, c.5, v.II, is referred to the head.

2. Batzar, Gold, is referred to Chokrnah, as though laid up in strongholds, Job, c.22, v.24, 25, and c.36, v.19.

3. Charutz, Prov., c.8, v.10, is referred to Binah, from the digging of it; which name belongs to the feminine gender.

4. Zahab Shachut, that is, fine and drawn Gold, 2 Chron., c.9, v.15, because it hath the analogy to the thread of Chesed.

5. Zahab, alone, is referred to Geburah, because gold cometh from the north, Job, c.37, v.22.

6. Paz, and Zahab Muphaz, are referred to Tiphereth, I Kings, c.10, v.18; Psalm, c.21, v.4, and 19, v.11 ; and Daniel, c.10, v.5. For so Tiphereth and Malkuth are compounded in the golden throne, I Kings, c.10, v.18; also when it is called a vessel of Gold, Job, c.28, v.17; a crown of Gold, Psalm 21, v.3; bases of Gold, Cant., c.5, v.75.

7. Zahab Sagur, is referred to Netzach, that is Gold shut up, I Kings, c.4, v.20, 21, Job, c.28, v.15, to wit, to bring forth seed.

8. Zahab Parvajim, is referred to Hod; 2 Chron., c.3, v.6, I Kings, c.6, v.20, from its likeness to the blood of young bullocks, for this kind is red at the left hand.

9. Zahab Tob, is referred to Jesod, that is good Gold, Gen., c.2, v.12, for this kind is called good, after the manner of a good man.

10. But Zahab Ophir, is referred to Malkuth, Job, c.22, v.24, for it is the name of a land (or earth) as called so from ashes. See also I Chronicles, c.29, v.4.

And now concerning the name Zahab, I will lead thee into the cave of the hidden matter, and will show thee the treasuries of Solomon mentioned in Nehemiah, c.13, v.13, viz., the Perfection of Stones, Exodus, c.26, v.6.

Come see! There are many places, to which Gold is referred, viz., Geburah and Binah, and other special places, where the species of Gold are disposed by one thus, by another other ways. But now I represent to thee the nature of Gold in Tiphereth.

Neither can you object out of the Zohar or Tikkunim. For know, that in this place ought to be understood Tiphereth, of the measure or degree of Geburah. And it is a great mystery, because Tiphereth commonly contains Iron under it, from whence we seek Gold.

This is the Sol or Sun of nature and art, whose lesser number is ten, the symbol of all perfection which number by Gematria also shows you the lesser number of Tiphereth likewise the word Atah belonging to the same in its lesser computation.

Mingle therefore Iron and Clay, Daniel, c.2, v.33, and thou shalt have the foundation of Gold.

This is that Gold, to which is attributed the notion of Tetragrammaton, Exodus, c.32, v.5, in the history of the calf, which was to be ground to powder, and thrown upon the waters, v.20, whence you shall see seven kinds of Gold immediately following one another in the work.

First, simple Gold, which is called Zahab barely; for it is truly Gold though not digged out of the earth; nor destroyed by the violence of the fire, but living, rising out of the waters ; sometimes of a black, sometimes of a yellowish, and often like a peacock's colour; going back of its own accord into the waters, and this may he called Zahab Saba, as though you should say, Sabi, the Gold of captivity, because it is newly captured, and shut up in its prison; where it keeps a fast of forty days and nights, that you know not what is become of it, Exodus, c.32, v.I ; for there is then no external appearance, even as Moses was hidden and they knew not what had become of him.

Secondly, it becomes Zahab Shacuth as though killed and slain, for it dies and its corpse putrefies and grows black: then it is under judgment and the shells rule it, and the powers of the name of 42 letters fulfil their time upon it.

Thirdly, but then follows Zahab Ophir, as though you should say Aphar, for it is of the colour of ashes; which time the twenty-two letters of the alphabet will determine for you.

Fourthly, it becomes Zahab Tob, because it is good to colour, though not of the colour of Gold, but Silver. This may be called Chethem. For it may be so called, according to Lam., c.4, v.I. How shall Gold be coloured with redness, and Hacchethem Hattob, i.e., good Silver be changed? And thence is referred that text in Job, c.22, v.24, and put it upon Opher, he would have said Opheret, Lead, Batsar, Silver, that is this white Gold. For from hence you shall have Silver. And to Silver when it shall be in the state of a stone, add Nachlim, rivers of metallic waters; from whence you shall have Ophir, that is Gold of Ophir, which was accounted the best. Now you shall have the number of the great name Ehejeh; for thou shalt possess, after twenty-one days, these things. If thou wilt now open thy treasure, open it ; but it shalt yet only give Silver as stones, I Kings, c.I0, v.27.

But if thou desire more, let thy Gold be,

Fifthly, Zahab Sagur, i.e., shut-up Gold : Let it remain in the prison, in the place of its maturation, in the bowels of the earth of the wise men all the time of the Decumbiture of Ezekiel, c.4, v.6. And thy Gold shall become the

Sixth, Jarak Rak, i.e. yellow Gold, like Zahab Parvajim. These are the thirty men, Judges, c.14, v.19, whom Samson slew. For this being done,

Seventhly, your Gold will be Paz and Muphaz and Uphaz; being strengthened to conquer and colour all imperfect metals.

This is that Charutz, that sharp pointed (or penetrating) thing; which Job, c.41, v.30, says ought to be cast upon clay, i.e., imperfect metals, that hath Cohach, power to produce Gold: for Tit and Cohach are of equal numbers. And make it to boil like a deep pot, a sea of thick metallic waters ; and it shall become like a vessel of paint : But after that it shall make the path to shine, v.31-32. Blessed be the name of the glory of his kingdom for ever and ever.

I write these things, I the insignificant one, according to my slender knowledge, who have earnestly sought out secret things, to the healing of all creatures. But that which moved me thereto is spoken in Sohar Heaesinu, fol. 145, cap. 580, concerning the office of a physician, that I should not desist from the good and right way until I should find the best medicine : And the words are these;

It is written, Deut., c.32, v.10, "He found him in desert land and in the waste howling wilderness; he led him to find the causes, and made him understand and kept him as the apple of his eye. And rightly because he hath compelled all the cortices to serve him." Thus far was it written in the book of Kartanaeus the physician. And then he drew from this text various observations necessary to a wise physician about the cure of the patient, lying in the chamber of sickness, Genesis, c.39, v.20, where the captives of the king may worship the lord of the world. For when a prudent physician comes, he finds him in the land of the desert, and in the wilderness of the howling solitude, which are as the diseases afflicting him, and finds him in the captivity of the king.

Here it may he objected that it is not lawful to cure him, because the Holy One, who is blessed for ever, hath caused him to be ill and as if a captive. But this is not so ; for David says, Psalm 41, v.2, "Blessed is he who considereth (the curing of) the poor ; the Lord will preserve him and keep him alive." For he is poor who lies in the house of sickness ; and if the physician be wise that Holy One, who is blessed for ever, loads him with blessings, in reference to him, whom he cures. That physician finds him in the land of the desert, that is ill, etc. And what is to be done for him ; Rabbi Eleasar hath told us : Hitherto we have heard nothing of that physician, nor of his book; except that once a certain merchant told me that be heard his father say, that in his time there was a certain physician, who having seen a patient, presently said, "this one will live and that one will die" ; and that it was reported of him, that he was a just and true man fearing sin; and that, if any man could not procure those things he needed, he would buy them for him, and freely supply his necessities ; and that it was said, there was not so nice a man in the whole world, and that he did more with his prayers, than with his hands. And when we supposed this man to be the very same physician, the merchant made reply, "Certainly his book is in my hands, having been left to me as an inheritance by my father; and all the sayings of that book are hidden in the mystery of the law: And in it we do find profound secrets, and many medicines ; which notwithstanding, is not lawful to apply to any, except to him that feared Sin, etc." Rabbi Eleasar said, "lend it to me". He replied, "I will, so as to show to you the power of the sacred light." "And you have heard" (said Rabbi Eleasar) "that Book was in my hands twelve months, and we found in it sublime and precious lights, etc., and we have found in it various sorts of medicines, ordered according to the prescriptions of the law, and the profound secrets, etc. And we said, blessed be the holy and merciful one, who bestoweth a share of wisdom upon men from the supernal wisdom." Thus far here.

These things moved me to seek the like good and secret books ; and from the good hand of my God I found that which I now teach to thee. And the camea of this metal is altogether wonderful, for it consists of six times six partitions, everywhere wonderfully showing the virtue of the letter Vau, related to Tiphereth. And all the columns and lines, as well from the bottom to the top, as from the right to the left, and from one angle to another, give the same sum and thou mayest vary the same ad infinitum. And the various totals always observe this principle, that their lesser number is always 3, 9, or 6 ; and again, 3, 9 or 6 and so on. Concerning which I could reveal many things to thee.

Now I add this example, which shows as the total of a line the number 216 of Arjeh our wonderful lion, 14 times, which is the name Zahab, Gold. Compute and be rich.

11	63	5	67	69	1
13	21	53	55	15	59
37	27	31	29	45	47
35	39	43	41	33	25
49	57	19	17	51	23
71	9	65	7	3	61

CHAPTER III

CHESEPH, Silver is referred to Gedulah on account of its whiteness which denotes Mercy and Pity. In Raja Meh. it is said that by 50 silver shekels, Deut., c. 22, v. 29, is understood Binah, Understanding, but when from 50 portals it inclines to the side of Gedulah--see the book Pardes Rimmonim, tract 23, c. I I.

Cheseph, Silver, in Metallic things Rabbi Mordechai writes thus:

Let the Red Minera of Silver be taken, let it be ground very finely; add an Ounce and a half of the Calx of Luna to six Ounces of it. Let it be placed in a Sand bath in a Vial sealed. Let there be given a small Fire for the first Eight Days, lest its Radical Humidity be burnt up. The second Week, one degree stronger; and the third yet stronger; and on the fourth, that the sand may not be red hot, but so that when Water is dropped upon it, it may hiss. Then on the top of the Glass, thou shalt have a White Matter, which is the Materia Prima or tinging Arsenic, being the living Water of Metals, which all Philosophers call dry Water, or their Vinegar. Let this be purified thus: Take of the Crystalline Matter sublimed; Let it be ground upon a Marble, with an equal part of Calx of Luna, and let it be put into a Vial sealed, and set in a Sand bath again, the first two Hours with a gentle Fire, the second with a stronger, and the third with one yet more violent, and increased till the Sand will hiss, and our Arsenic will be sublimed again, the starry Beams being sent forth. And since a quantity of this is required thou shalt augment it thus:

Take six Ounces of this, and an Ounce and a half of the most pure Filings of Luna, and make an Amalgama, and let them be digested in a Vial in hot Ashes, till all the Luna be dissolved, and converted into Arsenical Water.

Take an Ounce and a half of this Spirit, and place it in a closed Vial: Let this be put into hot Ashes, and it will ascend and descend; which heat continue, till it leaves off Sweating, and it lies at the bottom the Colour of Ashes. Thus the matter is dissolved and putrefied.

Take one part of this Cinereous Matter, and half a part of the aforesaid Water, let them be mixed and sweat in a Glass, as before, which will happen in about Eight Days; when the Cinereous Earth shall begin to wax white, take it out, and let it be imbibed with five Washings of its Lunar Water, and digested as before. Let it be imbibed the third time, with five Ounces of the same Water, and coagulated as before, for Eight Days. The fourth Imbibition requires seven Ounces of the Lunar Water. And the Sweating being ended, this Preparation is finished.

Now for the White Work. Take 21 Drachms of this White Earth, 14 Drachms of the Lunar Water, 10 Drachms of Calx of most pure Luna; mix them upon a marble slab and commit them to Coagulation, till they grow hard; imbibe it with three parts of its own Water, till it hath drank up this Portion; and repeat that so often, till it flow on a Copper Plate, made red hot, without Smoke; and then thou shalt have the Tincture for the White, which thou mayest increase by the means aforesaid.

For the Red, you must use Calx of Sol, and a stronger Fire; and 'tis a work of about four months. Thus this author.

Let this be compared with the Writing of the Arab Philosopher (Geber), where he writes very fully of the Arsenical Matter.

Chesed, in the Metallic Kingdom, is Luna, Nemine Contradicente. And so the Lesser Number of Gedulah is as that of Sama, or Sima. Silver is referred to in Prov., c. 16, v. 16, and c. 17, v. 3, and also Psalm 12, v. 7, and Job, c. 28, v. I. Silver is also found allotted to each one of the Sephirotic Decad, thus see the c. 38 of

Exodus, v. 17 and 19, where Silver forms the Chapiters of the Pillars representing Kether or the summit. While Silver is compared with Chokmah, in Proverbs, c. 2, v. 4, and to Binah, in Prov., c. 16, v. 16.

Gedulah is manifest out of the History of Abraham, where Silver is always preferred, Gen, c. 13, v. 2, and c. 23, v. 15, 16, and c. 24, v. 35, 53.

Geburah is shewed, when Silver is put in the Fire, Prov., c. 17, v. 3, and Num., c. 31, v. 21. Psalm 66, v.10. Prov., c. 27, v. 21. Isaiah, c. 48, v. 10. Ezek., c. 22, v. 22. Zech., c. 13, v. 9. Mal., c. 3, v. 3.

Tiphereth is the Breast of the Statue, in Dan., c. 2, v. 32.

Netzach is a Vein of Silver, in Job, c. 28, v. 1.

Hod are the Silver Trumpets, Num., c. 10, v. 2.

Jesod is found in Prov., c. 10, v. 20, and Malkuth, in Psalm 12, v. 6.

The Camea of this Metal represents nine times nine Squares, showing the same sum twenty times, viz., 369, and in its lesser Number 9, which all the Variations shew, though they should be a thousand times a thousand; because this Chesed (which is Mercy) endureth for ever. Psalm 136, v. 1.

37	78	29	70	21	62	13	54	5
6	38	79	30	71	22	63	14	46
47	7	39	80	31	72	23	55	15
16	48	8	40	81	32	64	24	56
57	17	49	9	41	73	33	65	25
26	58	18	50	1	42	74	34	66
67	27	59	10	51	2	43	75	35
36	68	19	60	11	52	3	44	76
77	28	69	20	61	12	53	4	45

Barzel, Iron; in the Natural Science, this Metal is the middle Line, reaching from one extreme to the other. This is that Male and Bridegroom, without whom the Virgin is not impregnated. This is that Sol, Sun or Gold of the Wise Men, without whom, the Moon will be always in Darkness. He that knows his Rays, works in the Day; others grope in the Night.

Parzala, whose lesser number is 12, is of the same account as the Name of that Bloody Animal Dob, a Bear, Whose Number is 12 also.

And this is that Mystical thing, which is written, Dan., 7, 5, "And behold another Beast, a second like unto a Bear, stood on its one side, and it had three Ribs standing out in his Mouth, between his Teeth; and thus they said unto it, Arise, eat much Flesh." The Meaning is, that in order to constitute the Metallic Kingdom, in the second place, Iron is to be taken; in whose Mouth or Opening (which comes to pass in an Earthen Vessel) a threefold Scoria is thrust out, from within its whitish Nature.

Let him eat Batsar, i.e., Flesh, whose lesser Number is 7, that is Puk, that is Stibium, whose lesser Number in like manner is 7.

And indeed much Flesh, because the proportion of this, is greater than of that; and indeed such a proportion as Puk, that is 106, bears to Barzel 239; such shall be the proportion of Iron to Antimony.

But understand the Flesh of the Lion, which is the first Animal; whose Eagle's Wings, and so much as is very Volatile in him, shall be drawn out, and it shall be lifted up, and by purifying be separated from its Earth or Scoria: And it will stand on its Feet; that is, shall get its Consistency, in a Cone; like a Man erect and with a shining Countenance, like Moses. For Enos and Moses in full writing by Gematria each give 351. And the Heart of Iron, [for the heart, Leb and iron, Barzel, in their least Number both give 5], (Mineral) i.e., the Tiphereth of Man Mineral shall be given to it.

For even the name of the Star belonging to this, is Edom, which hath the Connotation of a Red Man.

These things being done, the third Beast ought to be taken, which is as it were a Leopard, i.e., Water not wetting; the Garden of the Wise Men; for Nimra a Leopard, and Jardin in their lesser Number, make the same Sum, viz., 12, Such also is the Quickness of this Water, that is not unlike a Leopard upon that account.

And he shall have four Wings of a Bird upon his Back, the four Wings are two Birds, which exasperate this Beast with their Feathers, to the intent he may enter and fight with the Bear and Lion; altho' of himself he be volatile and biting enough, and venomous like a Winged Serpent and Basilisk.

And the Beast had four Heads; in which Words are understood four Natures lurking in his Composition, i.e., white, red, green, and watery.

And power was given him over the other Beasts, i.e., the Lion and the Bear, that he may extract their gluten or Blood.

From all these are made one Fourth Beast in the 7th verse, which is frightful, terrible, and very strong: For it casts forth so great Fumes, that at some times there is Peril of Death, if he be handled at undue time and place.

And he hath great Teeth of Iron, because this is one of the Parts and Materials compounding it; Eating and Breaking himself, and others to pieces, and Treading the Residue under his Feet. That is, of a Nature so violent, that by many bruisings and tramplings, he is as it were tamed at length.

And he had ten horns, because he hath the Nature of all the Metallic Numbers.

A little Horn, etc., for out of this is extracted the young King, who hath the Nature of Tiphereth (that is of a Man) but of the Nature or Part of Geburah: For it is that Gold which predominates in the Work of the Wise Men. Thus far the Preparatories.

And now the Beast is to be killed, and his Body to be destroyed and delivered up to the Fire to be burned, etc. For now follows the Regimen of the Fire. Concerning which elsewhere.

The Sword of the Illustrious Naaman is also related to the word Barzel.

Lancea; in the Study of the Metallic Natures, the History of Phinehas, Numbers, c. 25, v. 7, belongs to this place. By the

Fornicators are understood the (Masculine) Arsenical Sulphur, and the (feminine) dry Water unduly mixed, together in the Mineral.

By the Spear of Phinehas is meant the Force of Iron acting upon the Matter to cleanse it of Dross: By which Iron, not only is the Arsenical Sulphur killed, but also the Woman herself is at length mortified; so that the Miracle of Phinehas may be fitly applied here. See also the Targum on this Place, i.e., Numbers, c. 25, v. 7. For the Nature of Iron is wonderful, as its Camea (whose lines add up to 65 each way) shews.

It is here given: the Number 5, and its Square (i.e., 25) denote the Feminine Nature, which is corrected by this Metal.

11	24	7	20	3
4	12	25	8	16
17	5	13	21	9
10	18	1	14	22
23	6	19	2	15

CHAPTER IV

Bedil, Tin; in Natural Science, this Metal is not greatly used; for as it is derived by Separation, so its Matter remains separate from the Universal Medicine.

Amongst the Planets, Zedek is attributed to it; a white wandering Planet, to which the Gentiles applied an Idolatrous Name, mention whereof is forbidden, see Exodus, c. 22, v. 12, and a greater Extirpation is promised, Hosea, c. 2, v. 17, and Zechariah, c. 13, V. 2.

Amongst the Beasts, no Allegory is better applied to this metal than that, because of its Crackling, it should be called Chazir Mijaar, a Boar out of the Wood, Psalm 80, v. 14, whose Number is 545; which is not only made five times from 109, but in its lesser Number shews a Quinary, as the Name Zedek 194; which Numbers being added, make 14; and they make the Number 5, which twice taken is 10, the lesser Number of the word Bedil, by the two figures of 46 being added together. But five times ten shews the Fifty Gates of Binah, and the first Letter of the Sephira Netzach, which is the Sephirotic Class to which this Metal is referred.

In particular Transmutations, its Sulphurous Nature alone doth not profit, but with other Sulphurs, especially those of the Red Metals, it does reduce thick Waters, duly terrificated into Gold; so also into Silver, if its nature be subtilized into a thin water by Quicksilver which (amalgam) amongst others is made well enough by Tin.

But its viscous and watery Nature may be meliorated into Gold, if it be duly pulverized with the Calx of Gold through all the Degrees of Fire, for ten Days, and by degrees thrown upon flowing Gold, in the form of little masses, which also I am taught is to be done with Silver. But no man is wise unless his Master is Experience.

I add no more; He that is wise may correct Natures and help by Experiments where they are imperfect.

Kassitera, Tin; See Bedil's Camea, where the Number resulting from every side is Dal; representing the Tenuity and Vileness of this Metal, in all Metallic Operations.

$$
\begin{array}{cccc}
4 & 14 & 15 & 1 \\
9 & 7 & 6 & 12 \\
5 & 11 & 10 & 8 \\
16 & 2 & 3 & 13
\end{array}
$$

CHAPTER V

HOD, in the Wisdom of Nature, is of the Classis of Brass; for the Colour expresses the Nature of Geburah, which this Sephira contains. And the Use of Brass was for instruments of Praise and Music, I Chronicles, c. 15, v. 19. "And Brazen Bows were of Use in War." 2 Samuel, c. 22, V. 35, Job, c. 20, V. 24, and the like, Samuel, c. 17, v. 5, 6, 38.

But as Hod is encompassed with a Serpent, so Nechuseth --Brass is of the same Root with Nachash a Serpent.

'The Seventy Talents of Brass of the Oblation' Exodus, c. 38, v. 29, represent Seventy Princes; for about this place is the greatest Force of the Cortices or Shells. Whence in Hod is a degree of Prophetical Representation, as from the Root Nachash comes Nechashim, Enchantments, Numbers, c. 23, v. 23, and C. 21, V. I. But he that will be curious, may find, that Hod has a special Decad. So also in the History of Brass, from the Law, he may easily gather a Decad.

For may not that Oblation in general from which afterwards Vessels were made for the Tabernacle, Exodus, c. 38, v. 29, be referred to Kether, since all the other degrees spring from this.

Doth not the Laver of Brass, Exodus, c. 30, v. 18, shew the Nature of Chokmah, from which an Influx is let down to all the Inferiors? But the Basis thereof, which also was of Brass, is Binah; for Chokmah resides therein.

Afterwards the Brazen Altar, Exodus, c. 27, v. 2, with its Furniture represents the two Extremes, for the two Bars in the same place were covered over with Brass; and are as it were the two Arms, Gedulah and Geburah. The Body of the Altar itself,

Tiphereth. The four Rings of Brass, to the right and left are Netzach and Hod.

And the Brazen Net, which was instead of a Foundation, is Jesod.

And if you say, that the Altar was to be referred to Malkuth, according to the most common Opinion, which Altar may represent the Notion of a Woman: I answer, 'Tis true according to the general Distribution of the Tabernacle and Temple. But amongst the special Classis of Brass, where all things before incline to the Female, and so also Tiphereth, the Notion of the Male will not be so remote.

For there are yet Adne, Brazen Bases, Exodus, c. 26, v. 37, and c. 27, v. 10, which being as it were the bottom of the Tabernacle, have congruously enough the Nature of Malkuth.

He that would here trace these Mysteries more largely, might easily prolong his Discourse: But a wise Man will in short understand the Foundation.

The wonderful Camea belonging to the Classis of Brass, contains seven times seven Squares; and the Sum of each Line, whether Horizontal, Vertical, or Diagonal, are equal to each other, and to Tzephah .

22	47	16	41	10	35	4
5	23	48	17	42	11	29
30	6	24	49	18	36	12
13	31	7	25	43	19	37
38	14	32	1	26	44	20
21	39	8	33	2	27	45
46	15	40	9	34	3	28

As for Example, Here all the Columns make the same Tzephah, 175, as is to be seen above; for the first Column to the right, 4, 29, etc., makes 175, and so the rest to the last towards the left. After the same manner note the uppermost corner 22, (where is the Mystery of the 22 Letters) 47, etc., and ending with the number 4, where note the Mystery of the Tetragrammaton and so all to the bottom. Lastly, crosswise from the Angle between the East and South, to the Angle between the West and North, 4, 11, 18, etc., are 175, and from the Angle between the East and North, to the Angle between the West and South, viz., 22, 23, 24, etc., make all 175.

Therefore contemplate these things and thou shalt see an Abyss of Profundity.

Unless thou hadst rather allude to those Coverings, in which Brass was used, Exodus, c. 27, v. 2, 6, etc.

So if No. 1 be omitted, and you begin with line 2, there meets you the Sum Botzatz, I Samuel, c. 14, v. 4, writ defectively. If you begin with line 3, you will have the like Sum of 189. If you begin with line 4, then 196. If you begin with line 5, then 203. And so they ascend, exceeding one another by 7.

But if by a skip you dispose the Numbers 1, and 3, and 5, and 7, and 9, etc., then begin with which you will, you will observe the same Proportion. Also 1, and 4, and 7, and 10, and 13, etc. Also 1, and 5, and 9, and 13. This Septenary Net will always, from every Face, represent the same Sum, whose farther Use I should be able to open elsewhere.

Nechusheth, Brass, see Sohar Pekude, 103, 410, etc., and see Hod as above. Amongst the Planets Nogah, Venus corresponds to it. A necessary Instrument to promote the Metallic Splendour.

Yet it hath more the part of a Male than Female. For do not deceive thyself, to believe a white Splendour is promised to thee, as the word Nogah infers. But Hod ought to receive a Geburic Influence, and gives it also. O, how great is this Mystery.

Learn therefore to lift the Serpent up on high, which is called Nechushtan, 2 Kings, c. 18, v. 4, if thou wouldst cure infirm Natures after the Example of Moses.

CHAPTER VI.

CHOKMAH, in the Metallic Doctrine, is the Sephira of Lead, or Primordial Salt, in which the Lead of the Wise Men lies hid. But how is so high a Place attributed to lead which is so Ignoble a Metal, and of which there is so seldom Mention made in the Scripture?

But here lies Wisdom! Its several Degrees are kept very secret; hence there is very little mention made of it. But yet here will not be wanting examples of the particular Sephiroth.

For may not that which, in Zech., c. 5, v. 7, is called a Lifted up Talent of Lead, and brought from the deep, represent the grade of Kether? And that which in the same Chapter, v. 8, is spoken concerning the Stone of Lead, it sets before itself the Letter Jod, which is in Chokmah.

Then Ezekiel, c. 27, v. 12, Lead is referred to the place of the congregation, of which type is Binah.

And Amos, c. 7, v. 7, Anak, a Leaden Plummet, denotes the Thread of Chesed. For Anak, with the whole Word, hath 72 the Number of Chesed. But in Numbers, c. 31, v. 22, Lead is reckoned amongst those things which can abide the Fire, will be referred to Geburah.

But Job, c. 19, v. 24, graven with an Iron Pen and Lead are joined together, from whence you have Tiphereth.

But in Ezekiel, c. 22, v. 18, 20, there is the Furnace, of Trial, or of Grace, or Furnace of Judgment, in which also is put lead; hence, Netzach and Hod; for thence ought to flow a River of Silver.

And Jeremiah, c. 6, v. 29, the Furnace of Probation; out of which, by the means of Lead, good Silver is looked for. Is not the just Man, and he that justifies, Jesod (i.e., the Foundation)?

But if you seek the bottom of the Sea, look upon Exodus, c. 15, v. 10, where the Notion of Malkuth will occur.

This is that Red Sea, out of which the Salt of Wisdom is extracted, and through which the Ships of Solomon fetched Gold.

Ophereth, in the Doctrine of Natural things, is referred to Wisdom, for a great Treasure of Wisdom lies hid here. And hither is referred the quotation Proverbs, c. 3, v. 19. The Lord in Wisdom hath founded the earth; I say, the Earth, concerning which Job speaks, c. 28, v. 6, which hath Dust of Gold. Where, take notice of the Word Ophereth, i.e., Lead. This Lead, by a Mystical Name is called Chol, because therein lies the System of the whole Universe. For its Figure has below a Circle, the Sign of Universal Perfection, and over the circle is a cross formed of four Daleths, whose Angles meet in one Point; so you may know, that all Quaternity lies here, and the Quaternions of Quaternity: whether you refer to the Elements, or Cortices, or Letters or Worlds.

And in this Lead of the Wise Men, four Elements lie hid, i.e., Fire, or the Sulphur of the Philosophers; Air, the Separator of the Waters; the dry Water; and the Earth of the Wonderful Salt.

There are also hid in it the four Cortices, described in Ezekiel, c. I, v. 4, for in the Preparation of it there will occur to thee the Whirlwind, a great Cloud, and a Fire enfolding itself, and at length the desired Splendour breaks forth.

Also the Natural Sephira of the Tetragrammaton, and the Metal thereof, occurs to thee here. And you will naturally travel through four Worlds in the very Labour; when after the Faction and

Formation, laborious enough, there will appear the wonderful creation: after which thou shalt have the Emanation of the desired Natural Light.

And note, that the word Chol, whose Number is 50, multiplied by 15, according to the Number of the Sacred Characteristic Name in the Sephira of Wisdom, will produce the Number of Ophereth, i.e., 750.

Also the Kamea of that Metal is also wonderful, in which the Number 15, viz., the Name Jah, i.e., a form of Jehovah, in a Magic Square of nine Squares (because we are in the ninth Sephira) throughout all its Columns, shows itself after this manner.

4	9	2
3	1	7
8	5	6

The Planet Shabthai denominated from "Rest," because in this Principle is offered the most desired Rest.

And if you shall compute the words Lahab Shabthai, i.e., the point or edge of Saturn, there will arise the Number of the Name Ophereth; viz., Lead.

Arjeh, a Lion, in Natural Science is variously applied.

"For there is Gur Arjeh, a Lion's Whelp;" as Jacob speaks, Genesis, c. 49, v. 9. That word Gur, a Whelp, Numbers 209, and if you add the whole Word in the place of a Unit, it will be 210, which is the Number of the word "Naaman the Syrian, the General of the Army of the King of Aram," 2 Kings, c. 5, v. 1, by whom is Allegorically to be understood the Matter of the

Metallic Medicine, to be purified Seven times in Jordan, which many men, studious in Metallic Affairs, call Gur.

2. And that thou mayest the better understand this Matter, take the Lesser Number of this word Naaman, which is 21, this is equal to the Number of the Name of Kether, which is Ehejeh, 21.

3. The Number of Naaman, with the whole Word, is 211; to which another Name of the Lion is equal, Ari, 211.

4. And so also Arjeh, a Lion is equal in Number to the first word of that wonderful History, 2 Kings, c. 5, v. I. "And Naaman, etc." For this constitutes 216.

5. Moreover, the word Kephir, a young Lion, and Jerik, agree also in their Number; for each of them give 310. And now it is known in Metallic Mysteries, that at the very Entrance, we meet the AEnigma of the Lion of Green growth, which we call the Green Lion; which, I pray thee, do not think is so-called, from any other Cause but its Colour. For unless thy Matter shall be green, not only in that intermediate state before 'tis reduced into Water, and also after the Water of Gold is made of it, remember that this Universal Dry Process must be amended.

6. The other Names of Lions, are Lebi, which is a Lioness, according to Job, c. 4, v. II. The Whelps of the Lioness shall separate themselves; Ezekiel, c. 19, v. 2. "Thy Mother being a Lioness lay amongst the Lions;" Nahum, c. 2, v. 12. "A Lioness is there"; v. 13, "The Lion did strangle them for his Lioness."

Also Lish, which denotes a fierce Lion, with long straight hair: as found in Proverbs, c. 30, v. 30. These two Names, in their Lesser Numbers each contain a Septenary, for Lebi numbers 43, which gives 7, and Lish 340, which gives 7 also. To these the Name Puk, Stibium is equal, whose Sum is 106, and its lesser Number is 7, than which nothing could be more plain. Especially if the Sirname

29

of that Mineral be considered, when it is called the Hairy Servant, or he with long hair or Ruddy haired; with many like Names given to it.

7. There is yet another Name of a Lion according to the Masters of the Sanhedrim, in chapter II, fol. 95, col. I, i.e., Shachatz; which also the Targum uses; and Psalm 17, v. 12; its Number is 398, in its lesser Number it is 2. And the Chaldaic Word Tzadida shews the same lesser Number 2, being used in Targum, 2 Kings, c. 30, v. 30, Jeremiah, c. 4, v. 30, (instead of the Hebrew Word Puk, which is Antimony) for its sum is 109, which together with the whole Word, is 110, and its lesser Number 2.

8. At length also there, meets us the Name of the Black Lion, to wit, Shacal, whose Number is 338, and its lesser Number 5.

Now take the least Number of the word Naaman 210, which is 3, and the least Number of the Chaldaic word Parzel, Iron, which is 2, and you will have 5, the Black Lion.

9. Zahab, Gold, is called by the name Red Lion; and so not only the least Numbers of the Names Lebi and Lish make 14, which Number Zahab hath; but also the least Number of the word Zahab is 5, as I said but now to be equal to Shacal.

But under this Notion is to be understood Gold, either already Mortified, or now at length drawn from the Mines of the Wise Men,---Black in Colour, but Red in Potency.

CHAPTER VII.

JARDEN, denotes a Mineral Water, useful in the cleansing of Metals, and Leprous Minerals. But this Water flows from two sources, whereof one is called Jeor, i.e., a fluid, having the Nature of the Right Hand, and very Bountiful. The other is called Dan, Rigorous and of a sharp Nature.

But it flows through the Salt Sea, which ought to be observed, and at length is thought to be mixed with the Red Sea; which is a Sulphurous Matter, Masculine, and known to all true Artists.

But know thou, that the Name Zachu, i.e., Purity, being multiplied by 8, the Number of Jesod, produces the Number Seder, i.e., Order, which is 264. Which Number is also contained in the word Jarden; thus you may Remember, that at least Eight Orders of Purification are required, before the true Purity follows.

Jesod, in natural things, contains under itself Quicksilver; because this Metal is the Foundation of the whole Art of Transmutation.

And as the Name of El, doth insinuate the Nature of Silver, because both belong to the Classis of Chesed, (but here to that Chesed, which is inferior, viz., Jesod). So the name of El Chai, is the same as it were, Cheseph Chai, i.e., Quicksilver.

And so Kokab, a Star, is the Name of the Planet, under whose Government this Matter is, with the whole Word is 49; which same is the Number of El Chai.

But remember that all Quicksilver doth not conduce to this Work, because the sorts of it differ even as Flax from Hemp or Silk, and you would work on Hemp to no purpose, to make it receive the Tenuity and Splendour of fine Flax.

And there are some that think it a sign of Legitimate Water, if being mixed with Gold, it presently ferments. But the common liquid Mercury, precipitated by Lead, performs this. And what will it do ?

Verily I tell thee, there is no other Sign of a true Mercury but this, that in a due heat it invests itself with a Cuticula which is the purest refined Gold; and that in a little space of time, yea, in one night.

This is that which, not without a Mystery, is called Kokab, a Star; because according, to the natural Kabalah, Numbers, c. 24, v. 17, out of (the Metal) Jacob comes a Star; or in Plain language the shapes of Rods, and Branches, arise; and from this Star flows this Influence, of which we speak.

This Argent Vivre, in the Gemara Tract Gittin, ch. 7, fol. 69, is called Espherica, i.e., Spherical Water, because it flows from the Mundane Sphere.

And in Genesis, c. 36, v. 39, it is called Mehetabel, as tho' it were Me' Hathbula, by changing the order of the Letters, i.e., the Waters of Immersion, because the King is immerged in them to be cleansed.

Or as tho' it were the El Hatob, by a like Change of Letters; the Waters of the good El, or of Living Silver; for Life and Good have equal power, as Death and Evil have the same.

This is called the Daughter of Metred, that is, (as the Targum teaches,) the Gold-maker, Labouring with daily Weariness.

For this Water flows not out of the Earth, nor is digged out of the Mine; but is produced and perfected with great Labour and much Diligence.

This Wife (or female) is also called Me Zahab, the Waters of Gold, or such a Water as sends forth Gold.

If the Artist be betrothed to her, he will beget a Daughter, who will be the Water of the Royal Bath. Although some would have this Bride to be the Waters that are made out of Gold; which Bride (notwithstanding) poor Men leave to be espoused by great Men.

The Husband of Mehetabel is that Edomite King, and King of Redness, who is called Hadar, Glorious; viz., the Beauty of the Metallic Kingdom, which is Gold, Daniel, c. II, v. 20-29. But such Gold as may be referred to Tiphereth. For Hadar represents 209, which Number also the Tetragrammaton, multiplied by 8, produces, (which is the Number of Circumcision and Jesod) if the whole Word be added as one.

But that thou mayest know, that Tiphereth, of the degree of Geburah, is understood; know thou, that that Number being added to the whole, is also contained in Issac, which in like manner is of the Classis of Gold.

The City of that King is called Pegno, Brightness, from its Splendour, according to Deut., c. 33, v. 2. Which Name, and the Name Joseph, (by which Jesod is meant, have the same Number 156. That you may know that Argent vive is required to the Work; and that the Royal Beauty doth not reside out of this Splendid City.

To this place belongs another Sirname, i.e., Elohim Chajim, as tho' it were called Living Gold; because Elohim and Gold denote the same Measure. But so this Water is called, because it is the Mother and Principle of Living Gold: For all other kinds of Gold are thought to be dead; this only excepted.

Nor will you err, if you shall attribute to it another special name, for it may be called Mekor Majim Chajim, that is, a Fountain of Living Water. For, from this Water the King is enlivened, that he may give Life to all Metals and Living Things.

The Kamea of this Water is altogether wonderful, and exhibits in like manner the Number Chai (i.e. Living) 18 times, the same Sum in a Magic Square of 64 Squares, which is the Sum of Mezahab, Waters of Gold; being variable, after this manner, to infinity.

8	58	59	5	4	62	63	I
49	I5	I4	52	53	II	I0	56
4I	23	22	44	45	I9	I8	48
32	34	35	29	28	38	39	25
40	26	27	37	36	30	31	33
I7	47	46	20	2I	43	42	24
9	55	54	I2	I3	5I	50	I6
64	2	3	6I	60	6	7	57

Here you have the Sum 260, from the bottom to the top, from the nght hand to the left, and by the Diagonal; the lesser Number of 260 is 8, the Number of Jesod; as also the Root of the whole Square is 8.

The Symbol of the first Sum is 260, which makes the word Sar, i.e., "he went back," because in going forward the Sum always goes backward through the units.

For Example, if you begin with 2, reckoning the first Column for 8 the Sum will be 268, which is resolved in 7.

If you begin with the 3 (reckoning 8 for the second Column) the Sum will be 276, which resolves into 6. And so of the rest. And so also the number of Purifications increasing, the Weight of thy Water decreases.

CHAPTER VIII.

JUNEH, a Dove; amongst the AEnigmas of Natural things, the Name of a Dove is never applied to the Metals themselves, but to the Ministering and Preparing forms of Nature.

He that understands here the Nature of the Burnt Offering will not take Turtles, but two young male Pigeons, or Sons of the Dove, Leviticus, c. I, v. I4, and C. I2, V. 8, and c. I4, v. 22.

But count the word Beni 62, and 2 for a Pair of Doves, and thence is the number 64 of the word Nogah, which is the Name of the 5th amongst the Planets, and you shall go the true way. Else "labour not to be Rich; Cease from thy own Wisdom:" Wilt thou cause thine eyes presently to discern it? That will not be: But the Scholar of the Wise Men maketh to himself Wings, and flieth as an Eagle, even as he doth the Minerals of the Stars to heaven. Prov., c. 23, v. 4, 5.

Jarach, the Moon or Luna in the History of Natural Things is called the "Medicine for the White," because she hath received a Whitening Splendour from the Sun, which by a like shining, illuminates and converts to her own Nature all the Earth, that is the impure Metals.

And the place of Isaiah, c. 30, v. 26, "the moon shall be as the Sun," may be mystically understood of this, because the Work being finished, she hath a solar Splendour; but in this State, the place of Canticles, c. 6, v. 10, belongs to her,---" fair as the Moon."

By the same Name the Matter of the Work is called: and so indeed it is like to the crescent Moon, in the first State of Consistence; and like to the Full Moon in the last State of Fluidity and Purity. For the words Jarach, the Moon, and Razia, Secrets, also Rabui, a Multitude, have by Gematria the same

Numbers, because in this Matter are found the Secrets of Multiplication.

Gophrith is Sulphur; in the Science of Minerals this Principle is referred to Binah, to the left because of its Colour; and to left also, Gold is wont to be referred; and Charutz, a kind of Gold, is also referred to Binah, and being 7 in its lesser Number agrees with that of Gophritha.

Therefore the Gold of Natural Wisdom ought to be Charutz; that is digged out, or the like not excocted. And this is that Sulphur, which hath a fiery Colour, and is penetrating and changing to impure Earths; to wit, Sulphur with Salt, Deut., c. 29, v. 23. Sulphur with Fire, rained down upon the Wicked,---that is the impure Metals, Psalm 106, v. 6.

You must dig up this Sulphur; and it is to be digged out of the Water, that you mayest have Fire obtained from Water. "And if your Ways be right before the Lord, your Iron shall swim upon the Water," 2 Kings, c. 6, v. 6. "Go thy way then to the River Jordan with Elisha"; see v. 4. "But who shall declare the Geburah of the Lord?" Psalm 106, v. 2.

Many seek other Sulphurs, and he that hath entered the "House of the Paths" shall understand them, Proverbs, c. 8, v. 2. For the Sulphurs of Gold and Iron, the Extraction whereof is taught by many, and is easy; also of Gold, Iron and Brass; also of Gold, Iron, Copper and Antimony, which are gathered together after Fulmination by Vinegar, out of the lixivium, which are changed into a Red Oil, with a moist Hydrargyrum,---do tinge Silver. For from Proverbs, c. 21, v. 20, we know there is a Treasure to be desired and also an Oil to be found in the dwelling of a Man of Wisdom.

Finis.

www.ingramcontent.com/pod-product-compliance
Lightning Source LLC
Chambersburg PA
CBHW071752090426
42738CB00011B/2660